Naughty Nuts & Bolts

Creative Talents Unleashed

GENERAL INFORMATION

Naughty Nuts & Bolts

By

Creative Talents Unleashed

1st Edition: 2019

This Publishing is protected under Copyright Law as a "Collection". All rights for all submissions are retained by the Individual Author and or Artist. No part of this publishing may be Reproduced, Transferred in any manner without the prior **WRITTEN CONSENT** of the "Material Owner" or its Representative Creative Talents Unleashed.

www.ctupublishinggroup.com

Publisher Information
1st Edition: Creative Talents Unleashed
info@ctupublishinggroup.com

This Collection is protected under U.S. and International Copyright laws

Copyright © 2019: Creative Talents Unleashed

ISBN-13: 978-1-945791-64-2 (Creative Talents Unleashed)

Credits

Book Cover

Raja Williams

Book Introduction

Mark Heathcote

Creative Director

Mark Heathcote

Editor

All Authors Responsible For Own Work

Introduction

The theme of this anthology, isn't in any way compiled to shock our readers or to embolden our writer's hedonistic desires beyond the realms of the actual physical truth, but to quite simply tell us factually the particulars good or bad, hilarious or sad about themselves, about dating in our currently vastly changing world—about their sexual preferences experiences their carnal desires needs and to divulge them bravely, unblushingly, unashamedly to share them with us; what it is to date someone today or to fall-in-love or to never find love at all. Love is not a fantasy, but it can be magical. Naughty Nuts & Bolts takes a good look at these bodily functions through heart, mind and body and physically unparalleled expectations.

Mark Andrew Heathcote,
Author of *In Perpetuity* & *Back on Earth*

Table of Contents

Anticipation *Angela Bertoli*	1
Living Dream *Don Kingfisher Campbell*	2
Imaginary Lover *Branch Isole*	4
Wisp of Love *Ken Allan Dronsfield*	6
Green Eyed Monster *Tina Louise*	7
Self-Rejection *Paige Turner*	8
Midnight Passion *Stuart Kilmartin*	9
Mystic Universe *Hela Jenayah Tekali*	10
Heightened Tease *Baidha Fercoq*	12
Night *David Wagoner*	13
Fire Kisses Day *Heather Hazlett*	14

Hello Kitty   15
Peter V. Dugan

An Afternoon at the Ranch   17
Lyne Beringer

A Fairy-Tale Romance   18
Olfa Philo

Madness   19
Tina Louise

My Biggest Fear   20
Bevan Boggenpoel

Electricity   22
Don Kingfisher Campbell

Eye Contact   24
Lynn White

Sh**(shh...)   25
Antonia Valaire

Wanton Desire   27
Scott Thomas Outlar

Tell Me   29
Maggie Mae

She Said   30
Branch Isole

Final Stroke   31
Markus Fleischmann

Slipping on Love *Bevan Boggenpoel*	33
The Dance *Peter V. Dugan*	34
Her Work *Mark Andrew Heathcote*	36
Wholly Man *Jeff Santosuosso*	37
The Night the Earth Moved *Damon E. Johnson*	39
A Long Strange Trip *Jonathan Aquino*	40
Another Kind of Discovery *Nomthandazo Nxabela*	41
In Silence We Speak *Scott Thomas Outlar*	42
Baggage *Raja Williams*	44
That Place *Sue Lobo*	45
Kindred *Branch Isole*	46
Yes, You Are *Vernon Wade*	48

Perhaps We Should   49
Jill N. Pontiere

The Thought of You   50
Lopamudra Mishra

Diary of Don Juan   51
Ken Allan Dronsfield

Music Box   52
Heather Hazlett

Moments   53
Tina Louise

Breathless   54
Jill N. Pontiere

Illecebrous   55
Luna Love

Imapatience   56
Shilpa Kulkarni

Lover's Ooze   57
Valormore De Plume

Last Night I Heard Your Voice   58
Vernon Wade

Ocean of Love   59
Ken Green

Journey...   60
Bipul Banerjee

Bury Me Deep *Lynn White*	61
A Dance Begins *Maggie Mae*	62
Dash Board Cotillions *Brenda-Lee Ranta*	63
Merriment in Memories *Ken Allan Dronsfield*	65
By No Means *Mark Andrew Heathcote*	67
Beautiful Liar *Paige Turner*	68
Love Woman from another land *Don Kingfisher Campbell*	70
Temptation *Elizabeth Esguerra Castillo*	71
Restrain Me *Mark Andrew Heathcote*	72
Chances *Angela Bertoli*	73
My Prison *Paige Turner*	74
Do You Want to Play *Angela Bertoli*	75

The Landscape of Your Skin *Sue Lobo*	76
Enchanted *Valormore De Plume*	77
Animal Nature *Vernon Wade*	78
Attention *Maggie Mae*	79
After Nine to Five *Ken Green*	80
Pink Mascato Wine *Emory Oakley*	81
Craving *Luna Love*	83
First Date Anxiety *Glenda Higgins*	84
OMG *Markus Fleischmann*	85
First *Lopamudra Mishra*	86
Be taken by you entirely *Mark Andrew Heathcote*	87
Fuckless Loveless Sexless Sex *Luna Love*	88

To Hold Her — 89
Tiffany Jensen

Skin deep — 90
Jackie Chou

Omelets — 91
David Wagoner

Nippy In the Night — 92
Baidha Fercoq

Serenade Me — 94
Jeff Oliver

Loved into Bold — 96
Nomthandazo Nxabela

Sexsanity — 97
Markus Fleischmann

Little Black Dress — 98
Jeff Santosuosso

The Mountain Between Us — 99
Bevan Boggenpoel

Jenny — 100
Lyne Beringer

Sweaty — 101
Jeff Santosuosso

Quiet Canyon — 102
Ken Green

Anticipation

I sit waiting at the table,
Where you said we should meet.
My heart is doing double time,
And sometimes skips a beat.

My head is full of dreams,
Of what will come of this.
But silently I'm drifting off,
Into that dark abyss.

The one that got away,
The love that didn't last,
I watched as my evermore,
Strolled right into my past.

Shake those ugly thoughts off,
Don't give it so much time.
This is how the love game's played,
Just one more hill to climb.

Angela Bertoli

Living Dream

Today we flew
On the magic
Carpet of love

Her hair blown
Back by force
Of sexual winds

A smile so
Genuine I nearly
Asked us wed

Afterwards armed
Our eyes to
Hide blushing grins

And lay on
The puffy rectangle
Of an afternoon

Hands clasped inside
Each other's full
Body natural embrace

Coupling still here
Brows dripping lids
Closed in living dream

But we couldn't stop
Time from waking two
To step off heaven

For calm table

Creative Talents Unleashed

Conversation self-histories
To add to memories

Don Kingfisher Campbell

Imaginary Lover

Standing motionless,
Camouflaged
I disappear into the landscape
Watching you through the small window
as you glide effortlessly around the room

You dance and you tease
Always trying to please
Your imaginary lover,
Who is he?

Seeing you
before the mirror
Enjoying
the both of you
Devouring
your every move
The two of you
under the harvest moon

You dance and you tease
Always trying to please
Your imaginary lover,
Who is she?

You twist and you twirl
Arms in the air
Hands in your hair
Two shy girls
Seductively bare

You dance and you tease
Always trying to please

Your imaginary lover,
Might we become three?

Soon my love soon
Soon will two be
Harmoniously in tune
Two will become one my love,
Soon

You dance and you tease
Always trying to please
Your imaginary lover,
is it me?

Branch Isole

Wisp of Love

My spirit is one with yours; since
burning times and zealot's reign.
We have walked, talked, made love,
made war lived and died together.
I have burned at the stake with you,
and with rising smoke and ashes, our
souls flew together into the night sky.
Now, finally being reunited with you
after what has seemed an eternity,
I find myself back there once again,
thrown onto the fiery flaming pyre,
my soul slowly burned to oblivion.
You haven't the strength to fight
these overly pious tormentors, or
put out the flames about me; so
once again, I burn, my essence rises,
a wisp of love bequeathed ... I burn.

Ken Allan Dronsfield

Green Eyed Monster

Inside me lives a monster
from time to time it raises
it's ugly head

I'm not proud of this monster
in fact I am very much ashamed
I feel like I have no control over it
it comes out regardless if I want it to or not

It seeks to destroy all that I love
all that I hold dear

My monster is green
it lives in the darkest part of me
it surfaces when I am weak

It takes over my soul
so much so I am no longer recognized
by those who love me

Creating doubt and paranoia
turns me into someone I don't want to be

I have lived with this monster for so long
and I am so very tired of it
But try as I might I cannot make it leave

I do not envy those it seeks to devour
all I can do is apologize and hope for forgiveness
So here it lives in the darkest part of me
lying in wait to rear it's ugly head

Tina Louise

Self-Rejection

Although I really hate being single
The fear of rejection controls me
I get lost in the thoughts of what if . . .

What if he doesn't like me?
What if I am not pretty enough?
What if I am not his type?
What if I am not good enough?

I start feeling like I have to pretend to be what I am not.

Pretending to like his likes.
Pretending I look the way I look right now every day.
Pretending we have chemistry.
Pretending I deserve to be with him.

And so,
I cancel our date
There is no need to pretend.

Self-Rejection, keeps me single again.

Paige Turner

Midnight Passion

The hour is late; the door is open.
The streets are silent; the moon is crescent.
The sounds of footsteps peter softly
in the night's dark vacuum.
The lost souls of daytime meet beneath
the blackened sky of a moonlit stream.
Under the cloud of smog,
a lone wanderer walks with purpose.
She walks through the tall suburban buildings
of neon streets.
An escape to freedom; an escape from life.
As the sands of time fall,
she knows that freedom is ephemeral.
Their lives are not their own,
and they are bound to a world not this.
But, for now, in these moments, they come together.
They share a forbidden passion,
where there are no winners.
They share life, lust, and liberty; but nothing more.
This world of theirs is fleeting.
Its foundation is skin deep, and it cannot last.
Even with the knowledge of a world in flames,
they continue to meet.
Convinced of turning fire into water.
There are no Romantic heroes.
Only people.

Stuart Kilmartin

Mystic Universe

I have visited all places
But none to my taste
I made many encounters
Been to the temples of inspiration
But yours is the best
To eat the food of wisdom
I wandered in the deserts of loneliness,
Like a lost pilgrim looking
Desperately for the light

Then you hold my hand and take me to the Valleys of hope
There I learn the essence of love
And dwell in the mirage of eternity
Above the skies, my soul flew
To purge its melancholy
And tranquil its saddened grief
I bathed in your sacred river
And wore the garments of love
And saw the mystic face of desire

You lit the candle of my burning heart
I saw the glittering passion with eyes of my soul
The Moon illuminated the concealed curtain of my heart.
Light of love rose from the bosom of my blooming soul
From the breast of the sleepy universe
Angels intimately appear in the clear moon light

Dancing joyfully under the chorus of clouds while as lovers we breathe and merge into the oneness of the clear-sighted, mystic universe

Hela Jenayah Tekali

Heightened Tease

The erotic freshness
of autumn's breeze
upon my skin.
The swirling mix of tingles and aches
as your fingers graze
caressing and teasing my hips.

Overcome
in a dizzy sail
when your lips smoothly slid
and brushed my mouth
launching memories of sensual cascades.

The twinning of soul
and tension of flesh
a tantric dance of passion's lust
leaving us to slumber in a melded heap.

The crispness of autumn's seductive breeze
rekindles a youthful frenzy

… such tantalizing moments
caught in your tease.

Baidha Fercoq

Night

we gathered shooting stars

against the day
skipped moon stones on the obsidian sky
and sloshed the Milky Way

skimmed the spangled pool
enumerated the stars pointing to them one by one
used our hands as a rule

plotting constellations high
with hands entwined in secret patterns
when we made love in the sky

David Wagoner

Fire Kisses Day

We sensually tangoed as lovers do
Long past the setting of a fire kissed sun
In lyrical movements of bodies possessed
With the longing desire to dance as one

Beyond the walls of ballroom confines
We caressed the floor with wanton steps
In sync to our intimate choreography
Precise in rhythm, smooth as red lips

Imagined walls burst into flames
Ignited by the heat of our raging fire
Translating the tango horizontally
We surrender to our inherent desires

Throbbing hearts accentuate the beat
Staccato souls flow in passionate sashay
Lovers dancing closely upon tangled sheets
Swaying in the moonlight 'til our fire kisses day

Heather Hazlett

Hello Kitty

She listens from her seat, a nameless face in the crowd
as the poet reads, she becomes aroused
by every word, syllable and sound, every verbal image
portrayed and ingrained on her brain.

He is the one.

Sixtyish, lively and petit, the insatiable hunger awakens
her instinct, the drive to hunt younger fresh meat.

She is on the prowl.

During the break between the feature and the open mike,
she stalks, lurks in the midst of the mingling audience
and waits with the patience of a lioness hiding in the tall
grass.

The poet moves on, headed down the hall to the restrooms.
With silent stealth, she follows unnoticed.
The open mike begins and the hallway empties.
She lies in wait just outside the men's room door.
The unsuspecting poet exits and she strikes like lightning.

The cougar pounces on her prey and with a death grip
lip-lock, drags him into the ladies' room and once
inside she displays catlike quickness.
With one swift motion, she locks the door, with the poet
paralyzed, in shock and awe, resistance, futile, no escape,
he accepts his fate and capitulates.

She holds his undivided attention.

She claws and paws his body; nibbles on his neck, ears and lips.
He is her ball of yarn, her scratch post of desire.
Oohs and aahs, moans and groans emanate from behind the locked door.
And then growls of delight and purrs of contentment.
With a sigh and a kiss, she leaves the poet mauled like a trophy
toy, a dead mouse or small bird left by the kitchen door.
Satiated she smiles and says as she exits down the hallway,

"Now you have good material to write a poem about."

Peter V. Dugan

An Afternoon at the Ranch

Have a shot of whiskey
Or you can mix it in a drink
It'll loosen inhibitions
Change the way you think
Then come and find me barely dressed
In a room just down the hall
We can watch an in-home movie
Then have ourselves a ball
Or maybe we'll play dress up
Make the roles reverse
You are safe inside my playroom
Nothing's too perverse
Afterwards remember
To follow the exit sign
Book next month's appointment
Leave a Benjamin behind

Lyne Beringer

A Fairy-Tale Romance

you wake up every morning
to the lovely smile of the wall,
then the bathroom winks at you
such a seductive wink ...
once tempted, you find yourself
sneaking into the other rooms
to caress the sensual furniture...
after kissing & cuddling the
soft pillows and cosy blankets,
you're gripped by the
irresistible touch of the kitchen
where you have to massage
the insatiable dishes while
thinking about the available
ingredients to concoct the daily
bewitching recipe of happiness ...
meanwhile your soul is being rocked to and fro
with the musical voices of your civilized kids
enjoying silent games...
every now and then you & your partner
exchange romantic compliments about
the grocery list, the expenses, the bills or
the secret love affairs with the high-tech gadgets
which end up mostly with a heartfelt hug...
once the 'last supper' is consumed,
the perfume of the dustbin starts
tickling your noses, hence foreshadowing a
hot intercourse on the horizon ...

Olfa Philo

Madness

Barefoot into the mouth of madness I walk
shards of glistening glass tearing skin from bone
yet I don't stop, despite the pain
despite every nerve in my body screaming...STOP
my soul torn to pieces by a million hungry beasts
they feed on the morsels that once were me

who am I?
what am I?
I no longer know...

Just a red stain on the horizon
waiting to be washed away by the cold rain

Tina Louise

My Biggest Fear

When our eyes first locked
I was unsure
How to turn on the charm
In order to lure

A picture-perfect painting
I couldn't stop admire
Just an accurate pick up line
That's what was required

I had to have this canvas
To see it in my frame
Enjoy all its perfect lines
And give it my last name

Taking that first step
Became my biggest fear
As I walked over
I saw her drawing near

How'd you do miss
Looking really fly
I could have sworn
I've seen you with the stars in the sky

To my biggest disappointment
He was looking for his man
I turned around and walked away
As fast as I can

I never felt so humiliated
In my entire life

How could I ever
Make another man my wife?

Bevan Boggenpoel

Electricity

we are side by side naked
in our California pajamas

then we touch fingers to
fingers and toes to toes

our eyes open unlock each
other's awakened hearts

you slurp me into ready
for action attentiveness

I have to slowly enter
your moist charged body

gradually increasing speed
as a fleshy mushroom piston

wanting to go 88 miles per
hour to achieve time travel

seconds into the wet future
flowers explode in my head

a small geyser erupts from
my stilled encased penis

endorphins play around
the front of my sweaty mind

I can feel the factory tubes
manufacture more sperm

as I drive my woman to work
she massages my sticky thigh

and says you're my baby
maker my powerful honey

my hairs stand up a little
with her evocating voice

Don Kingfisher Campbell

Eye Contact

Look at me.
Hey, look at me.
I'm here
I'm real,
a real person
and I like you a lot.
You're really special.
Hey look at me,
look into my eyes.
Look at me!

How the fuck
can I look at you
when you keep
kissing my eyes closed!

Lynn White

Sh**(shh…)

I am a secret untold
I am a nude monument ready to be unveiled
I am a sacred scripture need to be read
Why be Sh** about it.

I am a secret that will unfold
I am a love symbol printed bold
A mystery that is puzzling
I am on demand available
Remanded
Requested and access granted.

In your bed, I lay naked entwined legs by four
Sacred areas disturbed
Kissing is compulsory touching leaves us both breathtaking
Romance is not pornography
It is Biology, Physics, Chemistry, Literature and
Geography
Why are we sh** about it.

I was never shy to share me
Never was I so blatant
Until I met you
When I met you
A part of me displayed never knew existed
A part of me never to be exposed
A part of my body, exit closed
Until I met you, my insecurities slowly drifted
I felt a yearning screaming inside of me
Together we display naked and nude.

I dare the spies to watch
Beyond our sheets uncovered

Not revealed
Not yet told
We were bold in each other's arms set free
A part of me never was to be touched
A part of me no one knew
A part of me a secret
Until I met you
My sacred was read
I ask, why be sh** about us?

Antonia Valaire

Wanton Desire

reflections scream
from the mirror

eyes roll up
hair pulled back

wet against my legs
driving deep inside

warmth is holy
calling me home

your garden grows
with planted seed

flesh on flesh
soul meets soul

electric spasms
lust in the bathroom

finish over the counter
start again in the shower

all the dirty thoughts

wash perfectly clean

there is no wrong
when every move is right

a space so tight
holds me in place forever

Scott Thomas Outlar

Tell Me

There are many things
A man can say
They are never better
Than when he is
Looking you in the eyes
Telling or asking
While his hands
His body
Are all about you
On you, in you
Surrounding you
Asking the questions
That form the desire
To keep him there
On you, in you
Surrounding you
Tell me, tell me now
Say it, say it again
Yes, yes just like that
And again
They are never better
Than when he is
Looking you in the eyes

Maggie Mae

She Said

"Here comes the good stuff,"
she said Almost in a whisper
just loud enough to hear

Free sample given and received
Time spent on her knees
Cool kisses fresh as a breeze
Oh how that girl could tease
and please

Fireman's cap highly exposed
cocked, loaded and ready to explode

Ever so slowly with her brass ring
Around his maypole shaft did she sing

Enjoyment from thumbs,
Fingertips, body parts
She titillated, even his heart

From head to toe and back again
she left his heads in a spin

She was one who knew her stuff
Never too little just enough
Almost in a whisper
just loud enough to hear
leaning against him on the bed,
"Here comes the good stuff,"
she said

Branch Isole

Final Stroke

I tried to chain you down
With harp strings and twine
But they broke in passing of time
Now tired from your struggles
It's time for you to rest
Come lay your head
Upon my knee
Indulge yourself of the flesh
As you stroke it slowly
Slowly, slowly
In time pearls of desire
Will hold you
Touch you
Kiss you
Let go the lust within you
Hold me
Tightly
Softly
Let's light a match
Burn this world to Ash
Hand in hand we will dance
Upon the flames of our desires
Don't hold back the thirst in you
Drink of me
Deeply, deeply
Feel the heat that burns in you
As I fall upon my knee
Gently kissing you
Within the folds that part of you
Slowly, slowly
I lay you down to dream
Drifting on desire's seas
Feel my reach in the depth of you

Deeply, deeply
Rocking like the ocean's tide
Growing stronger
Tighter, tighter
As we join together our lust
Bathed in desire
Stardust lovers

Markus Fleischmann

Slipping on Love

Steaming hot
In the shower
Watering –
The prettiest flower
Like yin and yang –
Intertwined
Your love
Has made me blind
Washing your back
And kissing your neck
Don't want to escape
Your love's attack
Rose petals strewn
Leading to the bed
I slipped on the tiles
And bumped my head
Towering over me
In facial shock
I wished immediately
I can turn back the clock
How embarrassing –
It made me feel
Even though she said
It's no big deal
On that spot
Lies a non-slip mat
Really cannot afford
To feel shit like that

Bevan Boggenpoel

The Dance

She struts on stage scantily dressed, black leather mini skirt
and matching vest.
Dyed raven black short hair, mirrored sunglasses and black
patent leather stiletto boots add to the act.
Her alabaster skin glows in the spotlight, a contrast of black
and white.

With a wave of cat o'nine-tails,
she's Donna Matrix tonight.
"You can spank me anytime, sweet heart."
She moves and groves, as she removes her clothes
seductively slow to the hard driving beat of rock and roll.
"You go girl!"
The sunglasses are tossed aside and there's a fire in her
eyes.

Button by button the vest opens to reveal her abundant
breasts bound in a sheer lace bra and after the mini skirt
is lost, a tiny G-string is left, it leaves nothing to the
imagination.
"Keep going honey."
She prances and dances across the stage to a pole,
swirls and twirls,
straddles the extension of imaginary manhood
with her legs and spins around,
locks her legs and hangs upside down.

Lo and behold,
the bra is gone and she's back down on the ground.
"Ooh yeah! That's what we wanna see!"
She gently pats her behind with the cat o'nine tails as she
bounces around, does a flip and a split.

"All right, all right, all—right!"
"You're killing me, princess!"
"Oh baby take me I'm yours!"

Dollar bills fill the stage.

The routine ends, she cleans the stage, dresses and visits the
patrons, leaving two buttons unbuttoned on the vest.
She smiles and pushes up her chest.
Everyone obliges and sticks a bill between her breasts.
She says, "Thank you."
And I wonder if she dances for the money
or the adulation of the crowd.
But, when she gets around to me, she says,
"Hi, Pete. Long time no see," and gives me a peck on the
cheek.

Peter V. Dugan

Her Work

Her workbench is a tale of art
Brushes of every size lay in wait
She says it's heaven to spoil her-self
Paint & pamper & decorate.

My job is to look my very best:
& to put out my chest, pose & smile.
Wink in the right direction if it-
Serves me well, I'll put you under my spell.

Hair blonde then purple & pink the next
Body inked. All is a canvas nothing is real
The hair the eyelashes, her teeth whitened
And even her face has had a peel.

An all over body tan straight from
A spray can, isn't it obligatory
To then carry a Pomeranian a-
Pekingese, a Shih Tzu in a Chanel bag.

'I wear Stuart Weitzman heels baby,
I've got status baby, to hell with you'.

Mark Andrew Heathcote

Wholly Man

Convertible Sunday morning
leftover from Saturday night,
she pulls her top open
waiting for a green light.

Newspaper in hand, walking home
to my sleeping wife,
yesterday's news leftover today,
walking because I lack the drive.

She looks at me Sunday morning,
confessing what she's done.
She looks at me not quite at church.
She thinks I am the one

to grant her absolution.
But I am no priest
And cannot grant a sacred solution –
No, not in the least –

to her Saturday night's acts.
That the look in her eye mentions.
No. To know them, yes, but to
absolve them is not my intention.

The paper crinkles in my hand,
whose grip is white-knuckle tight.
The steering wheel turns in her hand.
She wants to go to the right.

The light turns green.
Her thigh flexes, depresses the pedal.
She accelerates toward the church.

which will hear neither confession.

Jeff Santosuosso

The Night the Earth Moved

Engaged in intense sexual warfare
we are relentless in our quest to conquer
the thirst that lies between our thighs.
The lengthy battle of wills defies time and gravity
as the night finally whips our bodies into compliance.
The covers are now scattered all over the floor
the king sized mattress is bruised and tilted to one side
the huge bed frame is bent completely out of shape
and the both of us have been stretched beyond our limits.
We can only hope that our neighbours took refuge.

Damon E. Johnson

A Long Strange Trip

You took me from the city,
away from the lights,
so many things you showed me:
twin peaks of wuthering heights,
a forest of mystery,
and more wondrous sights
So we went into the woods
as you held my hand,
I left behind my childhood
like sailors leave the mainland,
and new things I understood,
though nothing was planned.
At times I was going faster,
but it was a game:
you and I were explorers
for a prize we will both claim
at last we crossed the borders
and blessedly, we came.

Jonathan Aquino

Another Kind of Discovery

I untouched,
Lead his head down gently
Toes curling
Lips cursing
Nourished by his spirit

And he
He without Inhibition,
Holds parts of me

His Tongue pulsates
Against the flow
Of my discovery

At the meeting of our eyes
Tremors rush through my kingdom
I surrender the crown of my thighs
For him to wear
Like jewels of wisdom
His tongue pulsating
Against the flow
Of my discovery

Nomthandazo Nxabela

In Silence We Speak

First kiss
tongue slips
innocent
until lips are bit

Shivers up
the spine
cause fits

Fingers caressing
flesh
undressed

Lights off
slide
unto abyss

Stumble
to the bed
and miss

Fall onto
the floor
instead

Bodies entangled
as souls

are wed

Sighs and licks and moans
take stage
no words are left
that need be said

Scott Thomas Outlar

Baggage

I dragged it with me . . .
every
    hurt,
        rejection,
            strain,
and every other fragile moment of disappointment

All of my past heartbreaks brought . . .
fear,
   disappointment,
        pain,
           anxiety,
and all the unhappy endings that go with failed relationship's

For years I buried all those feelings in. . . .
deep,
  quiet,
     forgotten,
        places
where I learned to forget the feelings and emotions related to heartbreak

Then suddenly one day you came along . . .
and
  my
    baggage
       is
         wide
            OPEN.

Raja Williams

That Place

That place-
We're entered & planted, by love & fire's hot reddened flame, Formed in heart, limbs, organs, a face & we are given a name, Where men once trod & softly dared to writhe, moan & groan, From where all babes passed, but now have long gone & flown,
That place.

That place-
Of cushioned velvets in rose-madder pinks & deep silken plums, Nectar, saline spume of ancient moonbeams & red seeping suns, For our daughters & sons, tight frightening portals of their birth, Entry into life & the long journey, taking them to worldly earth,
That place.

That place-
Where those sanguined gypsies & those behind the hidden veils, Are proved upon virgin handkerchief, to all those doubting males, The honour or the shame, of the abashed & newly wedded maid, Shamefully, her coy innocence & dignity, to entire world displayed,
That place.

That place-
Dark, & fragrantly perfumed, where all life's secrets gather deep, The eternal garden, where if used & abused, the sad flower weeps, But, in youth & with loving permission, joy in love is freely given, In tranquillity, it's now at long awaited peace & appropriately shriven,
That place.

Sue Lobo

Kindred

I plagiarize your vulgarity
hoping to titillate young girls
who know no better,
tasting four letter words
repeated to a blush and giggle

Heartfelt swoons
delivered to tickle ears
with nasty little thoughts
hoping to let on
to harden pulsation innuendos,
as legs cross and uncross
exposing thighs
and shaven pubescent vulvae lips

A-line uniforms trim and crisp
addressing each other as 'slut'
Fabricating bawdy Chaucer-esque tales
Whispering sophisticated ribaldry rail
as if twenty-something vamps
thirty-something scamps
forty-something tramps
or middle aged mothers
disguised as MILFs who share martinis
and cabana boy-toys

In unison they squeal with glee
trollops declared one and all
Sisterhood of vixens lining up
a daisy chain of flesh
matriculating repertoires on display
juicy fetish devoteés

fingers lightly paw scrota orbs
mouths laud salacious words
master's voice does intone
missies vie for mister's bone

Branch Isole

Yes, You Are

Why do you argue with me,
when I tell you how beautiful you are?
Why do you roll your eyes and say,
"No, I'm not."
as if I have no idea
what I see with my own heart?
You turn the stereo up
so loud a deaf kid could dance to it,
miming the lyrics with a provocative sneer on your lips
dancing like there is nothing else in the world
but you and the music.
The curl above your forehead,
bobs like the top-knot of a quail on the run,
your eyes are smoky and sparkle at the same time.
You can deny it all you want to,
but you had better believe
 I know what I am talking about when I say:
"Darlin' you are just as cute as a bug's ass."

Vernon Wade

Perhaps We Should

Won't you please sit awhile?
Take off your shoes, relax
I know your style
Here is your coffee
Sip slowly
Talk to me
What's your rush?
You're still my crush
Share the memories we created
Laugh with me
Cry with me
Sigh with me
Love me once again
Perhaps we should lock the door
Lay down together on the floor
And forget the world
Forever more
Perhaps we should

Jill N. Pontiere

The Thought of You

I slept to wake with thousand thought of yours,
Looming and weaving in dreams
Little fear
A tinge of excitement,
A surge of happiness,
Ready to bloom with your fragrance
Then I realized you are here
With me, closed in my closet
Living in cheers.

Lopamudra Mishra

Diary of Don Juan

I'm in lust with a sky that I've yet to see;
in love with people that I've yet to meet.
Because my darling, I'm a lost nightmare
dressed in the finery of a princely fantasy.
Whilst lonely lips await whetted kisses;
cool hands caress your trembling cheeks.
Time lives for graceless darker dreams;
queen of hearts vivid in a diamond flush.
Struggle on a chair with three wobbly legs
where will it lead, to a baseless love bared?
Amnesty now wanton in pious infected liars,
colors flickering as grace and piety ascend
fantasy begets harmony in dreams sighing.
Soft red lips warmed by darting tongues, fuel
the fires, down deep inside. Rough hands glide
around the full apple bottom, quivers and the
trembles awaken slowly as the blood is boiling.
Clothes are left where the gravity takes them,
rhythms of the old headboard tap out its song.

Ken Allan Dronsfield

Music Box

His heart beats faintly
Playing its melancholy song
Beating out the constant rhythm
Of all that has gone wrong

He can't hear that dreary song
That plays within his soul
Eventually he must hear the song
Or his spirit will never be whole

Pain and tears comprise the notes
Locked in the music box of his heart
He has forgotten the tune of his past
Forgotten the pounding of his heart

What, but love, could hold the key
To unlock the music he holds within
Allowing the chorus of emotions to flow
Letting the painful memories seep in

She turns the key, unlocks his heart
To heal, the music must flow free
The notes are heavy with regret
Still she knows this is how it must be

The dreary music has droned in this box
In the music box made of stone
She holds him close in her arms
He will never again face the music alone

Heather Hazlett

Moments

It's funny how we meet people and after a short time
it's like we have known them forever...

They have such an impact, we worry about losing them
they become part of our lives, we look forward to time with
them every day. we laugh together, cry together, tell each
other things we wouldn't normally share.

time... distance... circumstance... all seem irrelevant

We wonder if at some point in time did our souls cross
paths were we once more than friends?... in another life
maybe

For now though.. we have these moments

If that is all we will ever have… make them count
don't be afraid to live. To love... hold nothing back

For life is so very short and sometimes
moments are all we have

Tina Louise

Breathless

Your skin on my skin
I wonder how it would feel
Your tongue sliding up my neck finding my ear
Tracing heart shapes along the curves of my body
As I start to shiver
Breathing so heavy now
I lay here and close my eyes
The thoughts of you leave me breathless

Jill N. Pontiere

Illecebrous

How to I begin to tell
This magnificent creature
The depths of my love
How his very touch
Makes my body quiver
That his smile
Brightens my day
That the way he looks at me
Makes me feel so beautiful
That his presence
Has my heart racing
My blood pumping
And when he writes
Poetry upon my flesh
Leaving my entire
body and mind
In an orgasmic state
No words can explain
How he makes me feel
Except that this is
Truly Love

Luna Love

Impatience

Love me not like a masterful artist,
Rain on me with the madness of a deluge
Engulf me with the impatience of a tidal wave
Lust for me like the scorching earth
Till I melt away like a snowflake on your lips
Then let the slow dance begin
Let pearl beads trickle down silken skin
Move with me in timeless rhythms
Let the music of our hearts guide us
Far beyond, into galaxies of happily dying stars

Shilpa Kulkarni

Lover's Ooze

Drawing close,
radiance forms around us,
your shyness enchants,
sparkling blue gaze calls to me,
exciting the fiery dance.
Not by chance,
circling limbs vine as one,
breath's impassioned sync,
replace a raft of smothered words,
the magic's just begun.
Glistening head to toe,
in soft candlelight's glow,
passing hours spin wildly,
noticed not by lover's ooze,
this dance will go through dawn.

Valormore De Plume

Last Night I Heard Your Voice

I know you think I don't miss you when you're gone
and it's true,
I keep busy all day long
and fall asleep before I get to bed.
But last night I heard you call my name.
I woke up in the dark,
in bed,
alone.
I reached for you but found only tangled sheets
I swear that,
for just an instant,
before I was fully awake,
I felt your
skin.
I lay there, drowsy, thinking of you:
of your breasts,
and the curve of your back.
The sly of your grin and
the dark smoulder of your eyes.
But you weren't there.
I rolled over again
and went to
sleep.

Vernon Wade

Ocean of Love

Your need of me
finds my desire
not wanting to escape
natures riptide

The greatest depths
hold beauty never seen
a salty taste
never taken away

Raw passion flares
swales capture us
out of breath
still holding each other

My want of you
is a love willing
to hold the silent undertoe
of a raging sea

again and again

Ken Green

Journey...

The cave deep down,
In her pink glory,
Yearns for the traveller,
To come in.
Moist fragrances floating in anticipation,
While the wagons of cylindrical delight,
Enter the milky ways of flight.
The me in you and the you in me,
Taste mutual buds of erotic bites.
Just as the journey goes on in the deep,
The naked peaks,
Showered by sweaty pearls,
Dance to the symphony of orchestration heat.
Songs of sighs,
Cries of joy,
Hang on to clouds nine.
Empathetical the beat of drums,
Blow away senses to another world.
Where the newly discovered WE,
Climb miles of vertical peaks.
Zeniths conquered,
Now the flights descend.
A steady landing,
On the entangled mesh,
Of united limbs……

Bipul Banerjee

Bury Me Deep

Bury me deep in the tall meadow grass
and bury me deep in your arms.
Lie with me here in the sun ripening flowers
where the blue of the sky hides the clouds.

Bury me deep in your cool white sheets
and kiss my eyes and my mouth.
And as the warmth of your body flows in to mine
I'll bury you deep in my arms.

Oh, bury me deep beneath darkening skies
and hold me close to your heart.
And buried deep with our love complete
we'll sleep covered over in stars.

But the future lies with us heavy and dark.
It has bitter sweet memories of now.
With the tastes of the past buried deep in our love
the tastes of the future are sharp.

I can see both the stars and the blackness of night,
the blindness and brightness of love.
The past and the future cast shadows of time
so bury me deep in your love.

And bury me deep in the tall meadow grass
and I'll bury you deep in my arms.
And lie with me here in the sun ripened flowers
where the blue of the sky meets the clouds.

Lynn White

A Dance Begins

When you are
Suddenly there
Behind me
Eyes meeting
In the mirror
Heat penetrating
my whole being
From the look
in your eyes
Then your lips
Are on my neck
Your arms are
Around me
Pulling me tight
To your heat
Suddenly there
Right there
The dance begins
Penetrating again
Again

Maggie Mae

Dash Board Cotillions

How they lusted for
their versions of love at
the dash board cotillions
Dressed in their best
with nowhere to go;
fogging windows to the
strains of 'Love Hurts'

Hands clumsily groped
handfuls of breasts,
thighs and asses
Too hard kisses and
too loud moans from
inexperienced mouths;
sounds of rapture

Skirts pushed up, tops
pulled down, pants
too tight in the crotch;
dodging assaults of
stick shifts and arm rests
Throaty kisses; horny
pleadings for more

They lusted for their
own versions of love;
inhaling the scent of
Charlie and High Karate,
moving to the strains

of 'Love Hurts,' long
before the reality was

that it really did hurt.

Brenda-Lee Ranta

Merriment in Memories

Sitting on the front porch,
in a chair owned by many; loved by few.
My guitar sits on a wicker loveseat;
covered in a blue matte with white
polka dots. Spending years serenading
the little red-haired girl next door.
I often think about high school;
not lettering in sports; not really
trying hard for higher grades.
Always thinking about girls, fishing,
hiking, baseball, working and oh, did
I say girls? It would appear, anything
but school work.
The long, hot summers spent
riding my bike many miles to fish
and camp along the Taylor River.
Times in the green grass fields
making out with girls of the
"make love not war" generation.
I wonder, sometimes, how I
graduated at all. I watched old man
Perkins' cows wander all around the back
fields during Math class. Grazing by the metal
bleachers on the football field.
I watched the crows, flying in the
winds. Fighting to land, windblown
once again. Picking pieces of
a child's sandwich, or corn; always
one out there, mysterious to me.
The lovely blue sky, with white
billowing clouds looking like pillows
of marshmallow balloons gliding by
in the breeze. Merriment in a day dream.

Sitting by the window in English class
hoping to hear the geese in their grand
flocks flying V formations heading south
each autumn. I dream for the hunting
season; always ready for the weekend.
Retired now, sitting on the front porch,
living for the memories and hoping for
another breath, and those lucid dreams
of past conquests and failed marriages;
the cats are fighting in the barn once
again; my guitar waits patiently to sing.

Ken Allan Dronsfield

By No Means

… Her Stetson apparel had taken her thus far
Oh, how she wishes she were a Cinnabar moth
An eye-dazzling beauty wearing red silken, cloth
Black heels - rather than the protocol
Steel-toed work boots, this is what she internal, spoke.

But on-site she too behaves like some burly sexist, bloke
Shouting out the orders, ogling whistling - no joke!
She gives as good if not better, than she gets.
And they my friends aren't sweet vignettes
Quotes from the bible, but she's no regrets.

… Well, maybe only this one, the dress code.
Like lots of women, she wants to look her best, be glam
Sit on the bonnet of a JCB, a red hot siren.
'Read each passing man, his cardiogram'…
'Say look, lads, by no means is this woman who I am'.

Mark Andrew Heathcote

Beautiful Liar

He was a beautiful liar,
that's the plain and simple truth
But, she never saw it . . .

With a numb mind walking on auto-pilot,
She found herself in her bathroom
She glanced into the mirror and shook her head in disappointment

"What were you thinking?" she whispered to herself.

Without thought she shed her clothes
Dropping to the floor with a velocity of disgust
Falling to her feet and the ground she is rooted to

She reaches into the bath and plugs the drain,
She turns on the water
"Make it hot!" she thinks to herself

Her right leg lifting and stepping in
Her toes scorching in the water;
awaken her numbed state of mind
A tear slips down her cheek as she drops her ass into the steaming hot water

Flesh turning red from the scorching heat
She smiles as his scent is removed from her body

Her sins washed away and buried in her mind

Lesson learned,
He will tell you he loves you
Just so he can fuck you.

Because . . . He's a Beautiful Liar

Paige Turner

Love Woman from another land

Wears a black spandex bodysuit
With white stripes on the sides
And spells LOVE in bold letters

Her superpowers include
Hugging me in elevators
Holding my hand in restaurants

But when I drive her back
To our not-so-secret lair on
The outskirts of the commercial city

She really moves to take off
And rests naked next to me
On our private soft island

Where she likes to tug on my beard
Tongue kiss me into another state
Then slurp on my penis to force me

To feel something so strong
I have to penetrate her chamber
We slide and rock together

Until one of us cries out
Stops, moans, holds still
Exits to relax skin to skin

Endorphins flowing around
Our minds communicating
Using society's magical devices

Don Kingfisher Campbell

Temptation

His hazy silhouette I see by the fireplace,
Ignited by the warmth of our closeness
With desire oozing from the pores of our skins,
The night breeze a witness to our passion and oneness.

Hear my cries as I beg you to explore the depth of my ocean
Wild tidal waves washing us out of the shore,
Bringing our souls to a different realm, pleasuring the senses
Quenching the thirst for desire, giving in to the call of the flesh.

He brought me to a world far from what I have known,
Like when Eve discovered the poison of the Tree of Life
Gave in to temptation of the snake in Eden
And let Adam enjoy the naked truth.

Thunder and lightning awakened the flame within me,
When it came to pass and we both succumbed to a little death
This can be a taste of real paradise as we both found ourselves,
Engulfed in blissful ecstasy, satisfying our curiosity.

Elizabeth Esguerra Castillo

Restrain Me

Restrain me because I want to bathe in your sun
I want a southern moon to shiver on you
From the naked shadows, I cast over you
Restrain me I'm like an applecart toppled over
Soon, I will be showing you the core of my heart
How I've longed to touch you after dark
And trace the horizon that lights up in your eyes
Restrain me because I want to bathe in your sun
I want only for you, I hunger-for-you
There is no other star shines brighter than you.

Mark Andrew Heathcote

Chances

It started with smiles,
A mingling of souls.
It grew like a fire,
In haste, no controls.

I reached for you blind,
A frenetic ordeal.
Thinking of nothing,
But how good I feel.

The day turned to night,
We frolicked and rolled.
My mind wasn't there,
My heart had found gold.

Blissful dysfunction,
Thoughts swirling too fast,
I'm wondering now,
How long could this last?

Your lust is my passion,
Hands tight in my hair.
Wherever this goes,
I'll follow you there.

Angela Bertoli

My Prison

Regret fastens to me like a child needing their mother
Over and over I do not understand the decisions I make
I listen to the words "we are adults making grown up choices"
But in that moment, I abandon all sound decisions

Your touch feeds my hungry soul
I can't help but to let go . . .

Surrendering to become intimately yours
Every part of my body I allow you to explore
I get lost in the world of seduction
For a moment loving you as if there would be more . . .

My sexual frustrations gone out the door
Hunger pains released with an explosion inside
The feelings I feel, I cannot hide
Just for a moment you loved the ride

Back to reality moments later
Realization that he doesn't love me
All he did was fuck me
Allowing me to escape my prison once more . . .

Regret consumes me, and I shut the door.

Paige Turner

Do You Want to Play

Well looky here,
What's this I've found?
A brand new leash
To lead you around.

I tried it once,
Turned out alright.
Let me try again,
I'm needy tonight.

That little kiss,
In the proper place.
Grants me my wish,
Do you want to play?

I'll need some jewels,
And a bit of cash.
Make it come true,
I'll do as you ask.

Whoever knew,
The power I hold?
My loving touch,
Turns dreams into gold.

Angela Bertoli

The Landscape of Your Skin

I'll wend my way upon your skin, of pallid opal milk,
In satin slippers upon your roads, of pale watered silk,
Tiptoeing over every hill & curve, so elegantly arched,
Slaking thirst from hollows, in desire ardently parched.

With soft caresses I'll roam, slip & softly, I will slide,
In your nooks & crannies, I will deeply, & secretly hide,
Diving your warm pooled grottos, to wallow & to swim,
And dancing upon your being, I'll gently, & tenderly skim.

I'll sip sweet scented sweat, from all your perfumed pores,
Musky moist sumptuousness, all kindness of nature's laws,
I shall go following fleshy maps, of your undulating veins,
Sketched in royal blue, of embroidered webbed spun skeins.

I shall not mar nor scar your terrain, wherever I may rove,
I've no purpose to dig & delve, for treasure's pricey trove,
My footprints will not sear, the paths of your skin so thin,
I merely want to know landscapes, of your lovely pearly skin.

Sue Lobo

Enchanted

Your arrival is like unto the morning star.
Your radiance vaporizes my empty darkness.
Your warm smile opens blossoms of joy in my heart.
Your tender kisses turn my passion to fire.
Your supple skin thrills my caressing touch.
Your attractiveness intensifies my devotion.
Your impassioned charisma perfects me.
Your uniqueness enchants me.

Valormore De Plume

Animal Nature

She moves like a horse,
shaking her head and tilting it to one side,
looking back over a bare shoulder,
long, brown hair falling like a shiny mane across the other.
She shuffles in place atop finely muscled legs,
haunches rolling beneath her short, summer dress,
nickering conversation with her girlfriends.

Vernon Wade

Attention

It doesn't matter
All these mixed
Emotions I have
All that matters
Is I want you
At attention
So my eyes can see
That you want me
Then I will devour you
In all your glory

Maggie Mae

After Nine to Five

I walk, then break into Olympic run
unable to contain the longing I feel

Others can't imagine my hair down, no glasses
or what consumes me when I am home

I say and do things once surprising to me
now so natural with you, a thousand times

A silent shy tongue, now raw in the truth
of outspoken desires as your touch finds me

I more than give freely, I will also take
my lover equally willing to do the same

What's between us stays behind the door
our private sanctuary, secrets ours alone

after nine to five

Ken Green

Pink Mascato Wine

Pink Mascato,
a shitty rose wine
barefoot bottle
glasses with no legs
open mouths
add thirsty lips

purple boxer briefs
traded for black
lacy thong
result of truth or dare.

Another open bottle, now,
red stained lips
selfie stick,
drunk photographs
handcuffs
paddle
lingerie.
A sexy dance?

Truths spill from painted lips
'sexual escapades on a school playground'
blushing faces
'a naughty sex toy hidden in sock drawer'

lips fall onto mouths
and necks
and cheeks.
Another bottle
this time apple, instead of grape
bubbles form around wet tongue

he is a
pretty boy, with green cat like eyes
I give him winged eyeliner
kiss purple into his cheek
smile into his mouth
he calls ME
boy

blue dildo
strapped into black harness
he calls me daddy
we fuck
like we've never been anything but gay.

Emory Oakley

Craving

Here you stand naked before me
With your hardness in hand
My heart's pounding
As you take me over
My legs, aquiver
For I have wanted you for so long
I lick my lips
With my sinister tongue
While looking up
Into your devilish eyes
We have Lucifer blushing
One position, two position, more
Wall, bed, floor
Orgasm after orgasm
It's what I've been craving
Sweat dripping
Scratches on your back
raw and bleeding
Have me pinned face down
moaning and screaming

Luna Love

First Date Anxiety

She felt the bone of their contention
It stabbed her when she turned
As his face fell off the table
Into the depths of her despair

Ripping through her consciousness
Tearing up the hope
Killing off the budding love
Landing with a heavy thud

Is love, fear turned inside out?
Wishing for an angel
Forklift from the sky
Laughing as it held them high

She's really not his sister
His mother or his ex
Really, can't he see her?
Trembling as she sat

White light everywhere
Falling off the table
Crashing through her soul
Ragged blackened hole

Of caring, despairing
Troubled pairing
Parting, after starting
Nothing at all

Glenda Higgins

OMG

Restrain me
With your panties tied
Around my wrists
Punish my mind
With words of desire
Whip my flesh
With your tongue lashing
Take my sanity
With your mouth biting
Still the earth
With your body grinding
Lower me gently from this high
With your seductive eyes
Bathe me in your twilight
Keep me rising like the moon
Make me your midnight
Do as you please
Do as you desire
Unleash your erotic fire
But take heed
Upon my release
It will be you
To find yourself
On your knees

Markus Fleischmann

First

In the first encounter, I thought to make you mine,
In the first exchange of eyes, I am thine,
In the first conversation, you impressed me a bunch,
Throughout the night I keep on thinking a lot,
In my first poem, you are the queen,
Because of this each of my words sing,
The melody of your imposing grandeur in my rhyme,
In the first hour of the day,
your morning wish uplifts my mood,
It keeps me smiling all through the day,
In the first thought of mine, I see your face,
From the first day till today you only you reign my empty space.

Lopamudra Mishra

Be taken by you entirely

Even waterfalls can freeze amid their roars
How cold silence trickles during intercourse
Everything nudges my heart towards yours
But even a mountain river can change course.
Oh, how I love a piano concerto just before-
All the others join in with their own musical score
Those solo moments are oh so enthral
But I want an ensemble and a whole lot more.

I want to watch our shadows dance in silhouette
I want your kisses, your fingers to tickle my ivory
I want an orchestra to push me over the edge
I want to lose control, be taken by you entirely.
I'm not the kind of man who goes seeking a bordello
I want an encore when all is said and done.
I want torrents of music, a crescendo
I want movement, a crying mandolin, a dying swan.

Oh, how I love a piano concerto just before-
All the others join in with their own musical score
Those solo moments are oh so enthral
But I want an ensemble and a whole lot more.
Now you've kissed me, I feel I'm once again twenty-one
I'm learning how to play again my first musical marathon.
Oh, what a phenomenon you are
Does my music with you, registrar.

Mark Andrew Heathcote

Fuckless, Loveless, Sexless Sex

Hate being woke up to him
On top of me
I cringe and I cry
But he doesn't know
Cause he never turns on the light
I wouldn't call it making love
Because there is no love
I wouldn't call it fucking
Because even fucking has passion
There is no kissing
No lustful groping
I wouldn't even call it sex
It's just a dick poking a pussy
For 2-3 minutes
Then I roll over
And silently cry myself back to sleep

Luna Love

To Hold Her

Pulling her in, a bit rough, by the small of her back
she fits right in that spot against your chest, inside your
arms.

Leaning to one side she lifts herself, hands wrapped around
your neck and buries her face into your neck. You actually
feel her body let go of all that she carries alone.

She moans instinctively every time she is close like this.
You know her eyes are closed and her mouth smiling.
You know she's warm between her legs and if you were to
take this moment somewhere else, she would be wet for
you in a second.

You know she wants closer.
She wants under your skin, like you want under hers.
With arms around her, feeling her trust, you feel taken over
with emotion.

Your hand instinctively finds the hair at the base of her
neck and tugs- lightly....giving her chills and a laugh and a
kiss. And then, there are her eyes.
Bliss…

Your other hand cups her ass.
The first word you think when she falls into you like
this..."mine."

And yes. And yes and yes.
Her. It's her. Home.

Tiffany Jensen

Skin Deep

My love, offer no prelude
to what we're about to do—
no conversation,
no revelation
of our younger days,
no shouting answers
to trivia questions.
Don't even bother
to gaze into my eyes—
just guide my fingers
to your bare groin—
I want to feel its rubbery texture
watch your naked body
under the semi-light.
I'm here for one thing—
this exquisite hour
in complete silence—
hands stroking flesh,
eyes only asking
for skin deep beauty.

Jackie Cho

Omelets

I'm teaching myself to crack eggs,
with one hand,
Like a French chef.
I want to make my lover omelets
at midnight.

We had our days
of frenzied first love making.
Later, there was sweet, slow love,
And the wait for that test.
Beautiful mama nursing our child.

Busy days of parenting,
I arrived to a child's glad cries,
after a long difficult day at work,
making me forget the day.
Exhausted kisses and sleepy lovemaking.

Then the sweet selfishness,
of just us two again.
Midnight is due to chime.
Our time is measured.
My left hand is no use.
I want to make omelets,
at midnight,
one more time.

David Wagoner

Nippy In the Night

Quietly we scaled
the swimming pool fence
it was the night and lights were dim
as the moon glistened on the undulating water.

Barracks lined the street
adjacent to the pool
soldiers were busy inside
polishing boots and studying training notes.

We crept quietly behind the mesh fence
keeping a low silhouette
slowly undressing and savoring
tracing his outline
such rigid muscles.

A statue in a garden
a Greek God.

Autumn's wind chased the water
and ripples gossiped
no secret safe.

Temptation had placed a bet
and I was losing to pleasure's intent
stepping closer, brushing our bodies past.

We lowered ourselves into
and immersed our nakedness
into the fluidity of our act.

But, short-lived was all our tact
… the water, too cold
and that was that.

Baidha Fercoq

Serenade Me

You invite me
as you captivate
the fire burns so hot
there is no control
I won't hesitate
these passionate vivid thoughts
a massage is given
my heart beats hard
I caress
hearing the sweet symphony
of my hands across your chest.

Serenade me
as our souls connect
clinch me
until it all makes sense
embrace me
in this world and the next
serenade me
never let go
caress
serenade me
until there's nothing left.

Make all the madness
become replaced with us
ignore insecurities
with just one touch
catch the sweat
that runs down our necks
procreate the passion
when our bodies connect.

Serenade me
as our souls connect
clinch me
until it all makes sense
embrace me
in this world and the next
serenade me
never let go
caress
serenade me
until there's nothing left.

The fire between us
not many ever feel
when our bodies connect
the obvious clarification
that this is real.

Serenade me
as our souls connect
clinch me
until it all makes sense
embrace me
in this world and the next
serenade me
never let go
caress
serenade me
until there's nothing left.

Jeff Oliver

Loved into Bold

He makes me
Bold
Enough
To take off the clothes of my heart
And by then my curves
Are already his
I let him be the paint I wear
On this brittle canvas
I present me
To be
And
With each stroke
he lays-
He makes me
Bold
Enough
To spread my wings
As well as I did these legs
To welcome
Him in
And
A little bit of trust is conceived
With each thrust
A little bit of trust is conceived
Ay! He makes me Bold enough
To consider the idea
That maybe I could be loved

Nomthandazo Nxabela

Sexsanity

I love it when you
Punish me with your lust
I love how you whip
My flesh with your tongue
Like a cat-o-nine-tails
You strip me bare
With pleasure and sin
Make it hurt so beautiful within
Such an ache
A deeper burning
To be touched is my lonely yearning
Strangle me with your desire
Don't tell me what I want to hear
Whisper how I should feel
Blind me with erotic senses
Bite away my normality
Show me your sensual insanity
Drown me in your essence
Release me in your presence
Stir the fire burning
Just don't walk me to the gallows
Leaving me hanging
Dangling on this fantasy
Hung by ecstasy

Markus Fleischmann

Little Black Dress

Men don't ponder the physics of dresses,
knit, tight, stretching to describe her curves.
On a hanger, it's a girl's.
On her body, it's all woman
from hip to hip, breast to breast,
small of the back, scoop of the chest,
thighs outlined in black,
flowing like the color of hormones,
the color of dreams,
of the procreation of the species,
homo sapiens,
homo testosterone and spermatozoa,
Ben Franklin sexually active in his 70s,
Picasso in his 80s,
homo subconscious urges busting through
the doors of consciousness,
pure blackout

Jeff Santosuosso

The Mountain Between Us

This natural structure
Standing in between
Taking us back
To where we've been

Just in that moment
We realized
Falling in love took us
By surprise

Continuing still
The life we left
But holding onto
What we've been blessed

A second chance
To find what we feel
No matter the stakes
Or heavy ordeal

Love conquers
Our deepest fear
Despite us hurting
What we hold dear

The mountain between us
We are prepared to climb
Although it appeared
At the most awkward time

Bevan Boggenpoel

Jenny

I'm a doll…and my name's Jenny
Made of naughty nuts and bolts
Have you heard about what I can do
I run on just twelve volts
Lay me down or sit me up
On the bed or in the chair
Pretend I am your girlfriend
As you brush my long faux hair
I'll listen without speaking
To everything you say
Grunt and moan repeatedly
After you press play
Later you can hold on tight
Stroke my rubber skin
The ready light is blinking
In case you share me with a friend

Lyne Beringer

Sweaty

Sexed in a pool of patchouli and perspiration,
I am sheeted here like a mummy,
straitjacketed.
I cannot release my arms to hold my nose.
You had not washed your hair,
my passionate bitch, spinning my brain
in a wash of essential bodily fluids.
This is how we finish.
I care no more how we started.

Jeff Santosuosso

Quiet Canyon

Love is a chorus
until the grand finale
when the choir of two
succumb to silence
offering no encore
as the curtain
slowly closes
and the night
echoes their sighs

Ken Green

Creative Talents Unleashed

Creative Talents Unleashed is an independent publishing group that offers writers an opportunity to share their writing talents with the world. We are committed to fostering and honoring the work of writers of all cultures. Our publishing group offers writing tips to assist writers in continued growth and learning, daily writing prompts and challenges to keep the writers mind sharp, marketing and events, as well as a variety of yearly publishing opportunities. We are honored to be assisting writers in the journey of becoming published authors.

Creative Talents Unleashed

www.ctupublishinggroup.com

For More Information Contact:

Creativetalentsunleashed@aol.com

Website: www.ctupublishinggroup.com

Blog: www.creativetalentunleashed.com

www.ingramcontent.com/pod-product-compliance
Lightning Source LLC
Chambersburg PA
CBHW061332040426
42444CB00011B/2883